Bald Eagle

Eagles can fly up to 30 m.p.h. and can dive at speeds up to 100 m.p.h.
Bald eagles develop the characteristic white head and tail feathers by 4-6 years of age
Eagles live can 30 years or more in the wild.

Blue Bird

Bluebirds are one of the few thrush in the America. They have blue, or blue and rose beige, plumage. Female birds are less brightly colored than males.

Blue Jay

   Mostly blue, with a white chest and underparts, and a blue crest; it has a black, U-shaped collar around its neck and a black border behind the crest.

Cardinal

A distinctive crest on the head and a mask on the face which is black in the male and gray in the female. The male is a vibrant red, while the female is a reddish olive color.

Chickadee

Tiny, approachable bird with a short neck and large head, giving it a distinctive spherical body shape. Stark white cheeks contrast with black cap and throat.

Downy Wood Pecker

What is special about a downy woodpecker?
Image result for downy woodpecker.
Downy Woodpeckers are small versions of the classic woodpecker body plan. They have a straight, chisel-like bill, blocky head, wide shoulders, and straight-backed posture as they lean away from tree limbs and onto their tail feathers.

Gold Finch

Adult males in spring and early summer are bright yellow with black forehead, black wings with white markings, and white patches both above and beneath the tail. Adult females are duller yellow beneath, olive above

Mourning Dove

A graceful, slender-tailed, small-headed dove that's common across the continent. Mourning Doves perch on telephone wires and forage for seeds on the ground; their flight is fast and bullet straight. Their soft, drawn-out calls sound like laments. When taking off, their wings make a sharp whistling or whinnying

Baltimore Oriole

Adult males are flame-orange and black, with a solid-black head and one white bar on their black wings. Females and immature males are yellow-orange on the breast, grayish on the head and back, with two bold white wing bars.

American Robin

The robin is a small, plump bird. Its black beak is short and thin. Males and females look identical, sporting a brown back, white belly and red breast, face and cheeks. In contrast, juveniles are speckled gold and brown, only developing the distinctive red plumage in adulthood.

RUBY
THROATED
HUMMINGBIRD

Ruby-throated Hummingbirds are bright emerald or golden-green on the back and crown, with gray-white underparts. Males have a brilliant iridescent red throat that looks dark when it's not in good light.

sparrow

Male House Sparrows are brightly colored birds with gray heads, white cheeks, a black bib, and rufous neck – although in cities you may see some that are dull and grubby. Females are a plain buffy-brown overall with dingy gray-brown underparts. Their backs are noticeably striped with buff, black, and brown.